For Every Season

PIANO DUETS
(Four Hands at One Piano)

By
MONA COALTER

Lillenas PUBLISHING COMPANY

KANSAS CITY, MO 64141

C O N T E N T S

Church Year

Christmas

Lent/Communion

Easter

Thanksgiving

Missions/Evangelism

Alphabetical

4

What Child Is This?

SECONDO

Traditional English Melody
Arr. by Mona Williams Coalter

Like a lullaby

What Child Is This?

PRIMO

Traditional English Melody
Arr. by Mona Williams Coalter

Like a lullaby

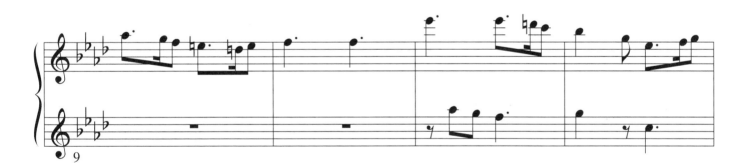

SECONDO

mel.

PRIMO

SECONDO

PRIMO

9

SECONDO

PRIMO

O Come, All Ye Faithful

SECONDO

From Wade's "Cantus Diversi"
Arr. by Mona Williams Coalter

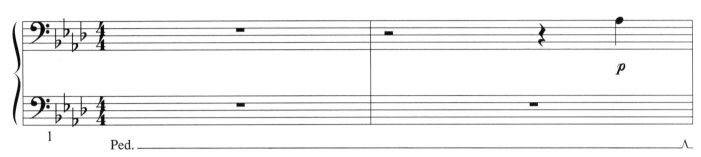

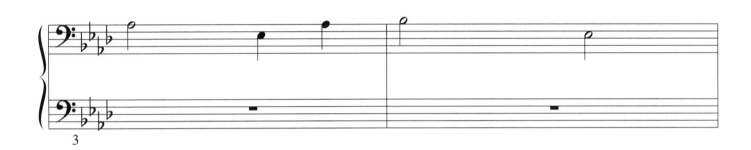

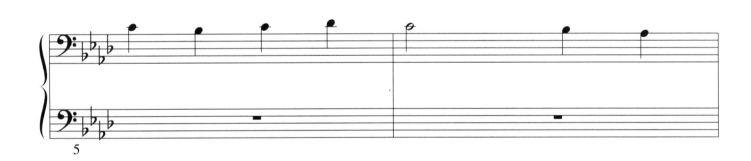

O Come, All Ye Faithful

PRIMO

From Wade's "Cantus Diversi"
Arr. by Mona Williams Coalter

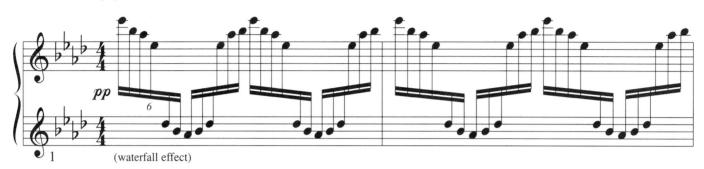

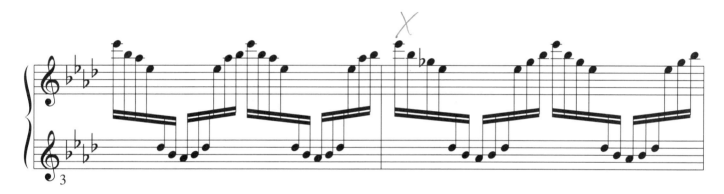

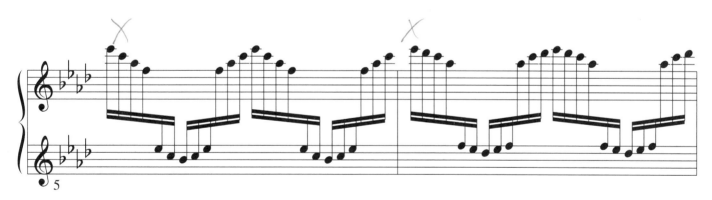

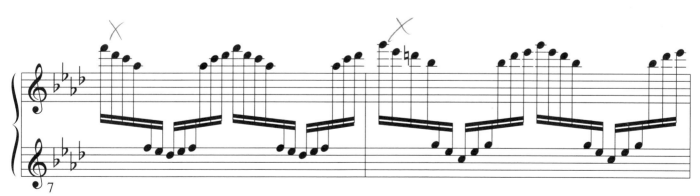

14

SECONDO

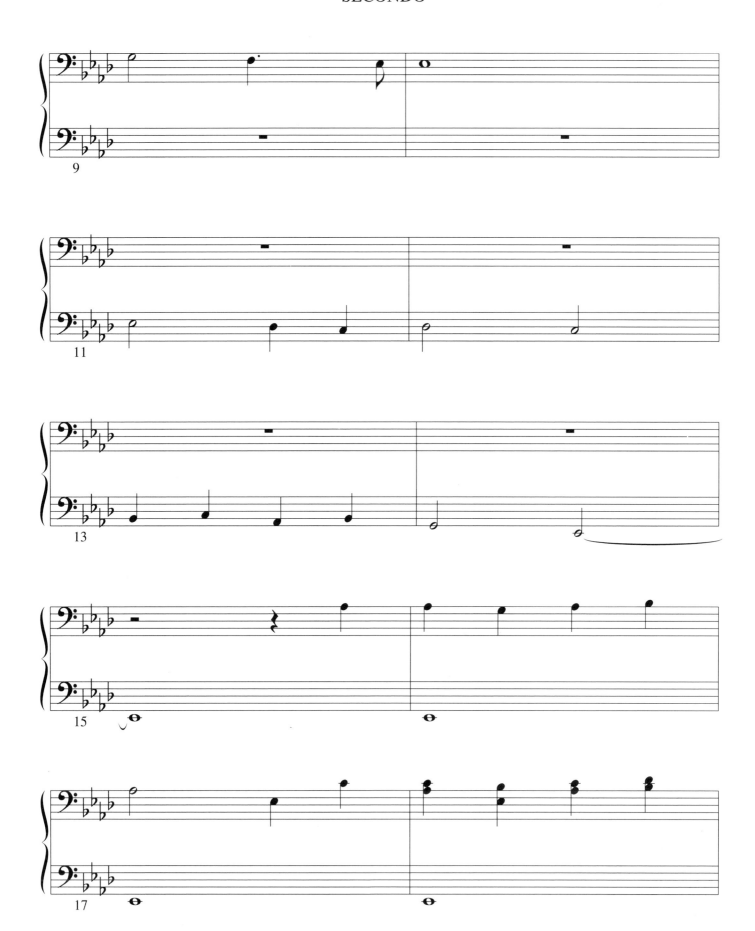

PRIMO

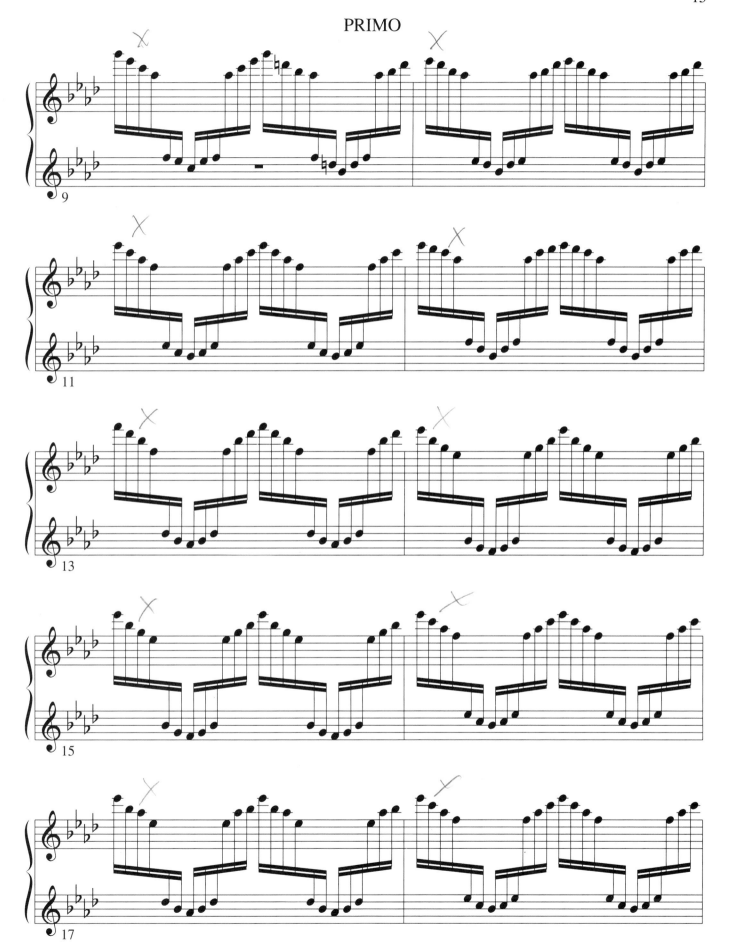

SECONDO

PRIMO

SECONDO

PRIMO

SECONDO

PRIMO

SECONDO

PRIMO

SECONDO

PRIMO

Majestic ♩ = ca. 112

SECONDO

PRIMO

Via Dolorosa
SECONDO

BILLY SPRAGUE & NILES BOROP
Arr. by Mona Williams Coalter

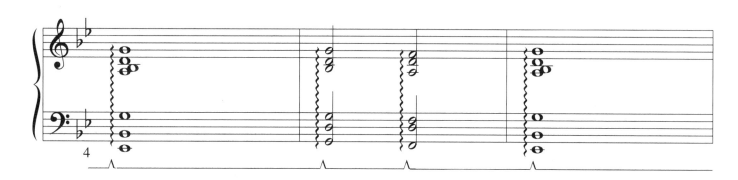

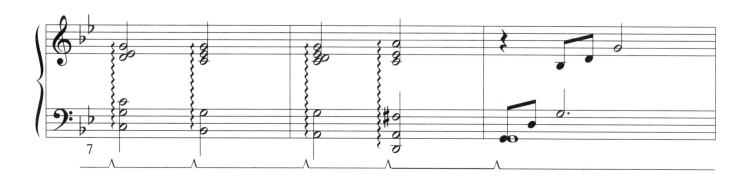

Via Dolorosa
PRIMO

BILLY SPRAGUE & NILES BOROP
Arr. by Mona Williams Coalter

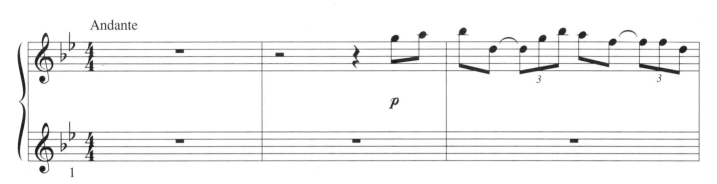

SECONDO

PRIMO

SECONDO

PRIMO

34

SECONDO

PRIMO

O Sacred Head, Now Wounded

SECONDO

HANS LEO HASSLER
Arr. by Mona Williams Coalter

O Sacred Head, Now Wounded

PRIMO

HANS LEO HASSLER
Arr. by Mona Williams Coalter

Andante con moto

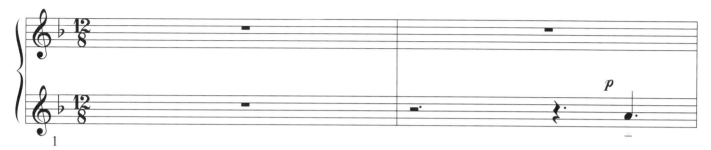

SECONDO

PRIMO

SECONDO

PRIMO

SECONDO

PRIMO

44

SECONDO

PRIMO

SECONDO

*Lower note of r. h. octaves optional until the F in measure 54

PRIMO

SECONDO

PRIMO

Easter Song

SECONDO

ANNE HERRING
Arr. by Mona Williams Coalter

Presto assai

Easter Song

PRIMO

ANNE HERRING
Arr. by Mona Williams Coalter

Presto assai

SECONDO

PRIMO

SECONDO

PRIMO

SECONDO

PRIMO

SECONDO

PRIMO

SECONDO

PRIMO

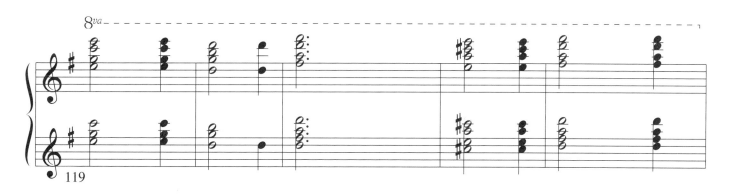

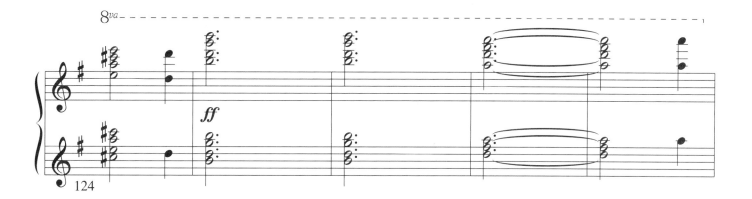

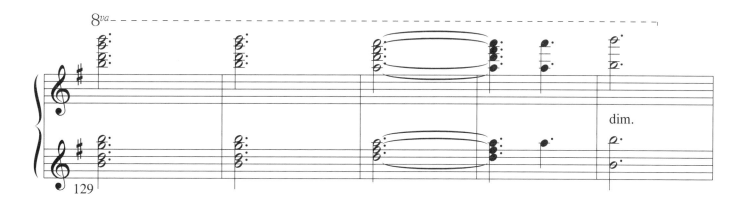

SECONDO

PRIMO

Christ the Lord Is Risen Today

SECONDO

From "Lyra Davidica"
Arr. by Mona Williams Coalter

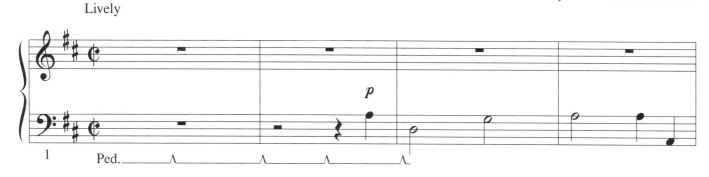

Christ the Lord Is Risen Today

PRIMO

From "Lyra Davidica"
Arr. by Mona Williams Coalter

SECONDO

PRIMO

SECONDO

PRIMO

SECONDO

PRIMO

SECONDO

PRIMO

SECONDO

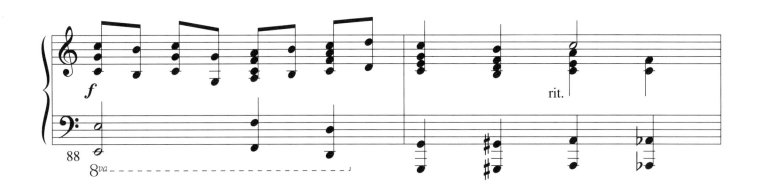

PRIMO

SECONDO

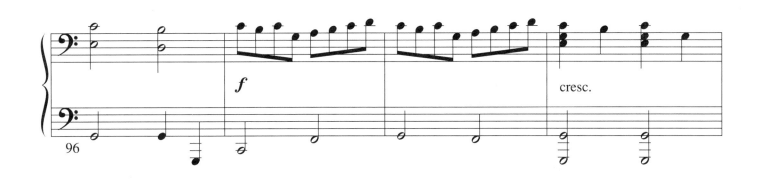

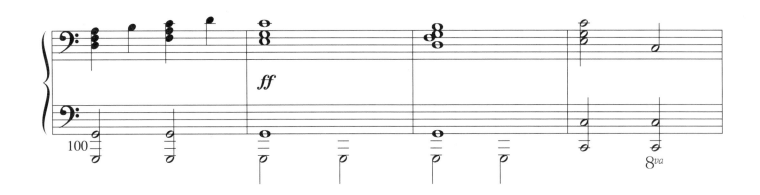

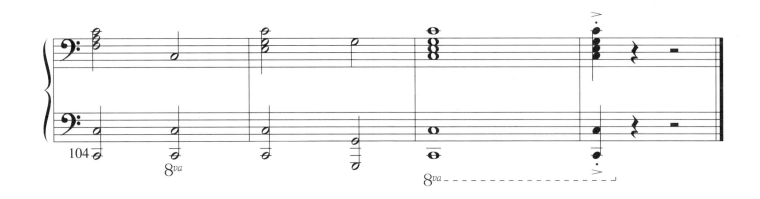

PRIMO

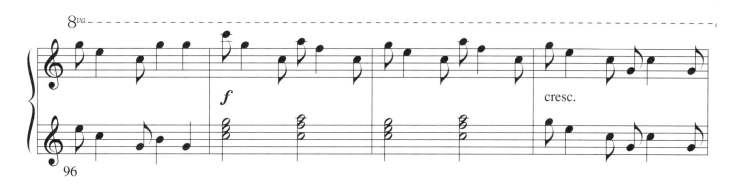

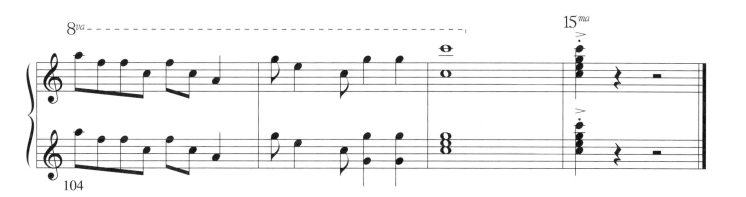

Now Thank We All Our God

SECONDO

JOHANN CRÜGER
Arr. by Mona Williams Coalter

Joyfully

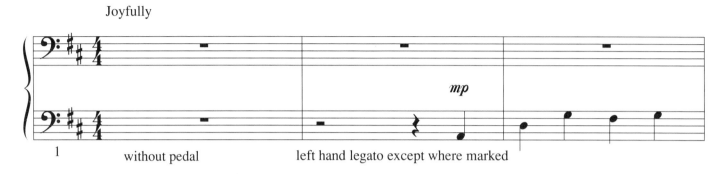

without pedal

left hand legato except where marked

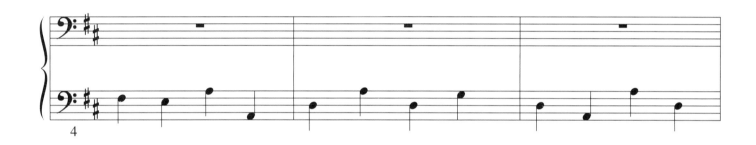

Now Thank We All Our God

PRIMO

JOHANN CRÜGER
Arr. by Mona Williams Coalter

SECONDO

PRIMO

SECONDO

PRIMO

SECONDO

PRIMO

SECONDO

PRIMO

SECONDO

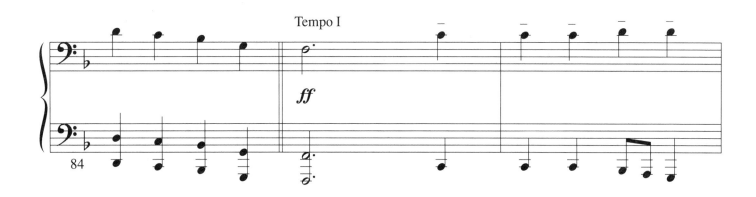

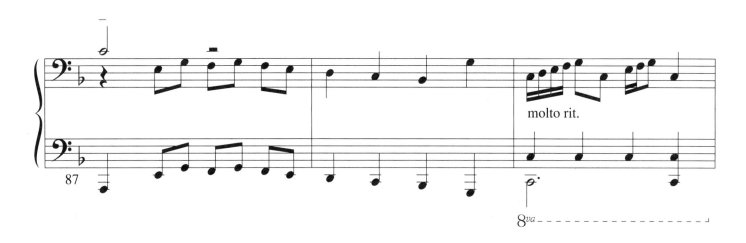

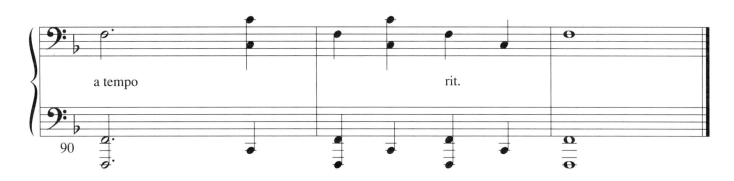

PRIMO

People Need the Lord

SECONDO

GREG NELSON & PHIL McHUGH
Arr. by Mona Williams Coalter

Moderato ♩ = ca. 96

People Need the Lord

PRIMO

GREG NELSON & PHIL McHUGH
Arr. by Mona Williams Coalter

SECONDO

PRIMO

SECONDO

PRIMO

SECONDO

PRIMO

SECONDO

PRIMO